THE DOMINICAN REPUBLIC

BY AMY RECHNER

DIOS PATRIA LIBERTAD

BLASTOFF! DISCOVERY

Blastoff! Discovery launches a new mission: reading to learn. Filled with facts and features, each book offers you an exciting new world to explore!

This edition first published in 2019 by Bellwether Media, Inc.

No part of this publication may be reproduced in whole or in part without written permission of the publisher.
For information regarding permission, write to Bellwether Media, Inc., Attention: Permissions Department, 6012 Blue Circle Drive, Minnetonka, MN 55343.

Library of Congress Cataloging-in-Publication Data

Names: Rechner, Amy, author.
Title: The Dominican Republic / by Amy Rechner.
Description: Minneapolis, MN : Bellwether Media, Inc., 2019. | Series: Blastoff! Discovery: Country Profiles | Includes bibliographical references and index.
Identifiers: LCCN 2018000617 (print) | LCCN 2018000875 (ebook) | ISBN 9781626178410 (hardcover : alk. paper) | ISBN 9781681035826 (ebook)
Subjects: LCSH: Dominican Republic–Juvenile literature.
Classification: LCC F1934.2 (ebook) | LCC F1934.2 .R43 2019 (print) | DDC 972.93–dc23
LC record available at https://lccn.loc.gov/2018000617

Editor: Rebecca Sabelko   Designer: Brittany McIntosh

Printed in the United States of America, North Mankato, MN.

TABLE OF CONTENTS

HISTORY UNDER THE SUN   4
LOCATION   6
LANDSCAPE AND CLIMATE   8
WILDLIFE   10
PEOPLE   12
COMMUNITIES   14
CUSTOMS   16
SCHOOL AND WORK   18
PLAY   20
FOOD   22
CELEBRATIONS   24

TIMELINE   26
DOMINICAN REPUBLIC FACTS   28
GLOSSARY   30
TO LEARN MORE   31
INDEX   32

ALCÁZAR DE COLÓN
SANTO DOMINGO

On a warm, sunny day a family explores the ancient town of Santo Domingo. They see 500-year-old Spanish-style buildings. Lively music plays in shops as they walk by. They visit the *Alcázar de Colón*, or the Palace of Columbus. The son of Christopher Columbus built it in 1510.

4

OTHER TOP SITES

AGUAS BLANCAS WATERFALL

CATHEDRAL OF ST. MARY OF THE INCARNATION

CAVES AT THREE EYES NATIONAL PARK

SAMANÁ BAY

Their next stop is the *Museo de las Casas Reales*, or Museum of the Royal Houses. The **tourists** marvel at **artifacts** from the Spanish settlers and the island's Taíno **native** peoples. Then, they enjoy fresh fruit smoothies at an outdoor café. History, beauty, and sunshine are all around. This is the Dominican Republic!

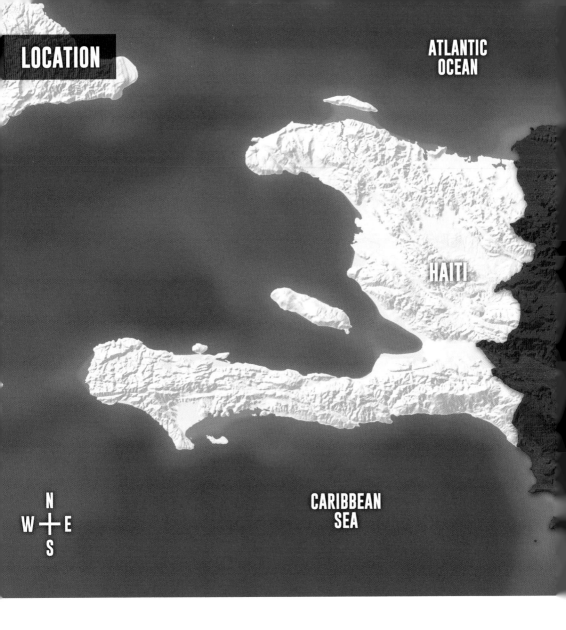

ATLANTIC
OCEAN

HAITI

CARIBBEAN
SEA

N
W ─┼─ E
S

The Dominican Republic is on the island of Hispaniola and
covers 18,792 square miles (48,670 square kilometers).
It covers the eastern two-thirds of the island. When combined
with the area of Haiti, the island is the second largest in the
West Indies.

PUERTO PLATA

SANTIAGO DE LOS CABALLEROS

DOMINICAN REPUBLIC

SANTO DOMINGO

LA ROMANA

MONA PASSAGE

COLUMBUS LANDS IN AMERICA

Hispaniola was one of the first places Christopher Columbus landed in December 1492. He thought it was Japan. Santo Domingo is the oldest city Europeans built in the Western Hemisphere that is still lived in.

The Dominican Republic's shores are washed by waves from the Atlantic Ocean to the north and the Caribbean Sea to the south. Puerto Rico lies 80 miles (129 kilometers) east across the Mona Passage. The capital city of Santo Domingo lies on the country's south-central coast.

LANDSCAPE AND CLIMATE

Four forested mountain ranges stretch across the Dominican Republic from east to west. The main mountain range is the Cordillera Central. It includes Pico Duarte, the Caribbean's highest peak. Squeezed between the mountain ranges are lowlands of dry grass and shrubs and valleys of **fertile** farmland. River systems flow down from the mountains into valley lakes and the Caribbean Sea.

PICO DUARTE

= CORDILLERA CENTRAL

MONTAÑA REDONDA

TRADE WINDS

The cooling wind that blows from northeast to southwest is called a trade wind. It was named by sailors who needed that wind to sail their trading ships westward.

SANTO DOMINGO

Average seasonal highs and lows

JANUARY
HIGH: 84 °F (29 °C)
LOW: 72 °F (22 °C)

APRIL
HIGH: 82 °F (28 °C)
LOW: 73 °F (23 °C)

JULY
HIGH: 95 °F (35 °C)
LOW: 82 °F (28 °C)

OCTOBER
HIGH: 88 °F (31 °C)
LOW: 79 °F (26 °C)

°F = degrees Fahrenheit
°C = degrees Celsius

The Dominican Republic has a mild **tropical** climate. The country's mountains and occasional northeast winds keep temperatures cooler. Heavy rains fall in the northeast. Hurricanes are a threat from August to October.

Much of the Dominican Republic's wildlife has been hurt by **habitat** loss. But the island is still home to a number of **diverse** species. The remaining forests provide shelter for bright birds like parrots and parakeets. Blunt-headed tree snakes slide among the trees. The rare rat-like hutia and Hispaniolan solenodon dwell in the forests and on rocky hillsides. Dwarf geckos, giant tarantulas, and rhinoceros iguanas creep about.

Pelicans, flamingos, and herons wade through **lagoons** and coastal waters in search of food. Humpback whales, turtles, and bottlenose dolphins swim offshore.

BLUNT-HEADED TREE SNAKE

BOTTLENOSE DOLPHIN

PALMCHAT

HISPANIOLAN GIANT TARANTULA

A TRILLING CHIRP

Palmchats are the national bird of the Dominican Republic. They are only found on the island of Hispaniola. The palmchat's chirp is a loud trilling sound.

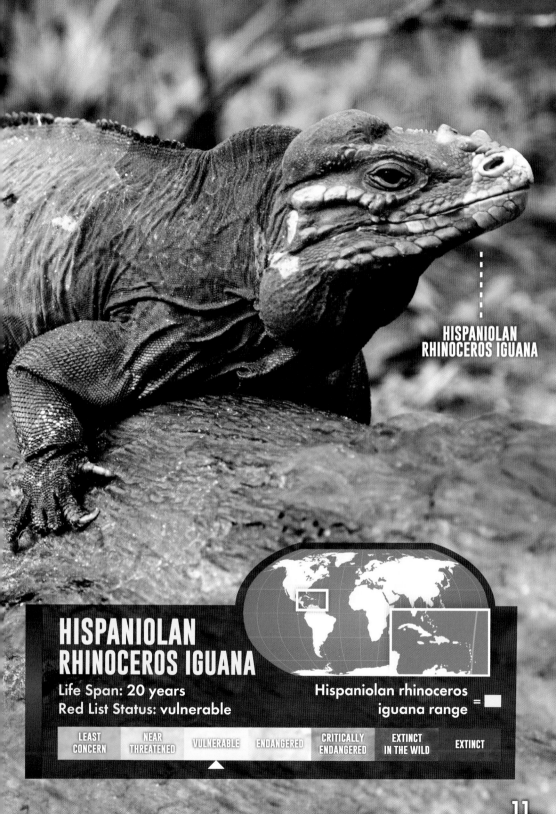

HISPANIOLAN
RHINOCEROS IGUANA

HISPANIOLAN
RHINOCEROS IGUANA

Life Span: 20 years
Red List Status: vulnerable

Hispaniolan rhinoceros
iguana range = ▪

LEAST CONCERN	NEAR THREATENED	VULNERABLE	ENDANGERED	CRITICALLY ENDANGERED	EXTINCT IN THE WILD	EXTINCT

A NEW HOME

The tiny town of Sosúa was settled by Jewish migrants. They fled Nazi Germany in 1940. They built the town and started successful farms.

Most of the Dominican Republic's 10.7 million people are the **descendants** of the European settlers and African **slaves**. Many have both European and African roots. There are small Arab, Jewish, and Asian populations, too. A community of **migrants** from Haiti has also made its home there. The country's official language is Spanish.

Dominican life is shaped by family and religion. Most Dominicans are members of the Roman Catholic faith. Many have blended it with other spiritual practices. Some people follow the African practice of vodou. It is called Gagá in the Dominican Republic.

FAMOUS FACE

Name: **Al Horford**
Birthday: **June 3, 1986**
Hometown: **Puerto Plata, Dominican Republic**
Famous for: **Power forward with the Boston Celtics, supporter of anti-bullying, reading programs, and WildAid**

SPEAK SPANISH

ENGLISH	SPANISH	HOW TO SAY IT
hello	hola	OH-lah
goodbye	adiós	ah-dee-OHS
please	por favor	pohr fah-VOR
thank you	gracias	grah-SEE-ahs
yes	sí	SEE
no	no	noh

SANTO DOMINGO

Rural villages are often built around a church and shops. Several generations of a family may share a home. Houses are made of wood or cement. They may have metal or **thatched roofs**. Cooking is often done outside to keep the houses cool.

Farming jobs are hard to find, so many people now live in cities where they can find work. People often live in crowded neighborhoods. The increased population has made apartment living common. Walking and bicycling make it easier to get around the busy streets. There are also mini-buses and taxis. Santo Domingo has a subway that goes north-south or east-west.

Dominicans are warm and welcoming. Most people greet each other by shaking hands. Close friends and family exchange hugs and kisses. People use lively gestures and share humor and laughter.

Social time is important in Dominican life. Guests are always welcomed with generosity and delight. Since spending time with family and friends comes first, being late for appointments or work is often okay. Dominican manners reflect their Hispanic **heritage**. They are respectful and friendly. One way they show this respect is by addressing older people as Don or Doña. It means sir or madam.

WORDS WITH HISTORY

Although the culture of the Dominican Republic is mostly Spanish, the Taíno language lives on. Many Taíno words have made their way into English, like canoe, Caribbean, potato, and hurricane.

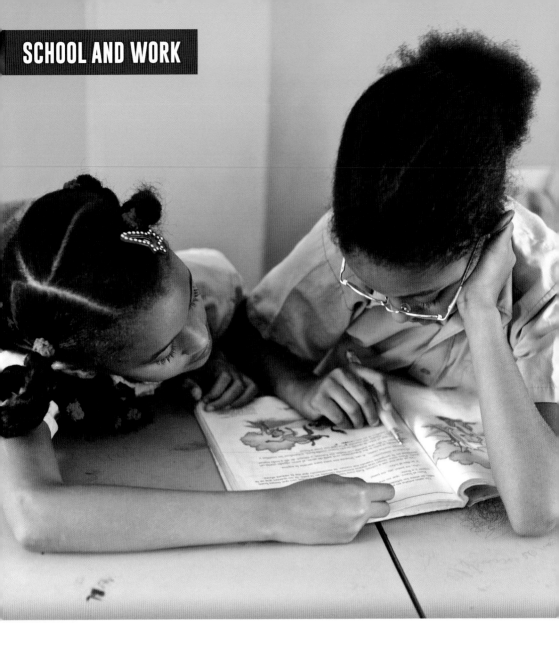

Education depends on location and wealth in the Dominican Republic. Rural areas only have a few schools. But primary school is free to all children ages 7 to 14. Middle and secondary school follow for those who can afford it.

Dominican farming produces fruit, coffee, and cacao. Large farms grow cotton and sugarcane. Factory workers process sugarcane into sugar products. **Textile** workers make clothes like cotton t-shirts and pants. Most Dominicans work in **service jobs**. Tourism is the largest employer of service workers. Others may work in government and housekeeping. Many travel to the United States in search of work.

CATAMARAN OPERATOR

THE MOST DELICIOUS PLANT!

Cacao is an important crop in the Dominican Republic. It is a dried seed found inside a hard, yellow pod. It is the basic ingredient in cocoa and every other chocolate product.

BASEBALL

The Dominican Republic's summerlike weather allows people to spend their free time outside. Baseball is the national sport. Dominicans cheer for their favorite professional teams and enjoy playing pickup games with friends and neighbors. Many Dominican baseball players go on to play on major league teams. Boxing and basketball are other popular sports.

FEEL THE BEAT

The music of the Dominican Republic has a strong African influence. Merengue is a dance as well as a kind of music. It has a strong beat from a two-sided drum called a tambora.

Music and dancing are enjoyed night and day. In the cities, people visit clubs to listen to live music and dance. Many dance parties come together in the streets when musicians begin to play. Friends and family gather to chat and play games like dominoes.

DOMINOES

EL PAÑUELO

What You Need:

- 8-10 players divided into two equal groups
- a piece of light cloth like a scarf, or a plastic bag
- a playground with enough room to run
- chalk

How to Play:

1. The two groups stand facing each other at a distance of 60 feet (18 meters). Each side counts off so everyone has a number. One person stands in the center on a chalk line dividing the playing field. They hold the scarf by a corner.

2. The person in the middle calls a number. Both children with that number run toward the middle and stop on either side of the line. Each try to take the scarf without an error. Crossing the line or touching the runner from the other team are errors. Both errors will give points to the opposite team. The fun part of this game is tricking the other runner into making errors!

3. Once a child grabs the scarf, the child from the other team can chase them back to their team's starting line. A point is earned when the child reaches their team's line with the scarf. If they are tagged before reaching the line, they lose the point.

4. The first team to reach the agreed upon number of runs, wins!

Dominican food combines the flavors of African, Spanish, and Taíno **cuisine**. Rice and beans are the base for most dishes. Pork and chicken are popular meats when they are available. Fruits like mangos, papayas, and guavas are locally grown and enjoyed at every meal.

MANGU

TRES LECHES CAKE

Breakfast is often *mangu*, or mashed plantains, and coffee with sugar. The national dish, *La Bandera*, often appears on tables for lunch. It features rice, red beans, meat, and salad. Dinners are light and may include eggs, fruit, or leftovers from lunch. Desserts include fresh fruit or custards and cakes like tres leches.

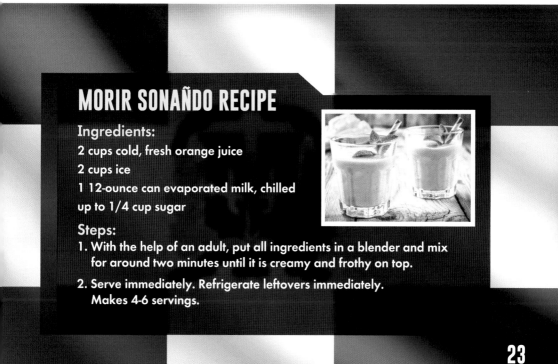

MORIR SONAÑDO RECIPE

Ingredients:
2 cups cold, fresh orange juice
2 cups ice
1 12-ounce can evaporated milk, chilled
up to 1/4 cup sugar

Steps:
1. With the help of an adult, put all ingredients in a blender and mix for around two minutes until it is creamy and frothy on top.
2. Serve immediately. Refrigerate leftovers immediately. Makes 4-6 servings.

CELEBRATIONS

CARNIVAL

The entire month of February is a long celebration called Carnival. It honors the Dominican Republic's independence and the beginning of the Catholic season of Lent. Villages enjoy parades, costumes, music, and dancing every weekend. February 27 is Independence Day and the most important day of festivities.

Semana Santa is Holy Week. It is a quiet week of prayer and worship. The week ends on Easter Sunday. Families celebrate by enjoying beach time together. Haitian and African **traditions** are celebrated during Semana Santa, too. Local Gagá drum celebrations welcome spring with music and dance. Other festivals honor **patron saints**, national heroes, and the rich culture of the Dominican Republic!

GAGÁ CELEBRATION DURING *SEMANA SANTA*

800–200 BCE
Waves of the Taíno people inhabit the Caribbean Islands, including Puerto Rico, Cuba, and Hispaniola

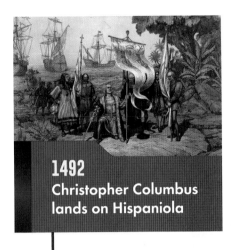

1492
Christopher Columbus lands on Hispaniola

1697
Spain gives control of the western third of Hispaniola to the French

1844
Dominicans declare independence from Haiti

1822
Haitian soldiers enter the Dominican Republic and make the island one country

1916–24
United States occupies Dominican Republic

1930–61
Rafael Trujillo becomes dictator and stays in control until he is killed by a traitor of Trujillo's state

1998
Hurricane Georges causes billions of dollars' worth of damage to the Dominican Republic and surrounding islands

1962
After 30 years under the rule of Trujillo, the Dominican Republic holds its first general elections

2012
Hurricane Sandy causes billions of dollars' worth of damage to the Dominican Republic and surrounding islands

Official Name: Dominican Republic

Flag of the Dominican Republic: A centered white cross divides the flag into four rectangles of red and blue. The white means salvation, the blue stands for liberty, and the red for the blood of heroes. A small coat of arms featuring a shield is in the center. A blue ribbon above the shield displays the motto, DIOS, PATRIA, LIBERTAD, which means God, Fatherland, Liberty. Below the shield is a red ribbon proclaiming REPÚBLICA DOMINICANA.

Area: 18,792 square miles
(48,670 square kilometers)

Capital City: Santo Domingo

Important Cities: Santiago de los Caballeros, Puerto Plata, La Romana

Population:
10,734,247 (July 2017)

COUNTRYSIDE
19.4%

WHERE
PEOPLE LIVE

CITY
80.6%

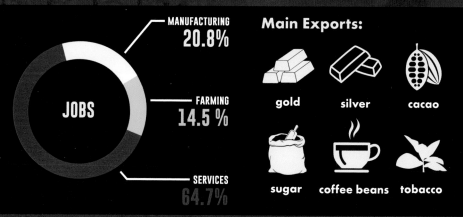

MANUFACTURING
20.8%

JOBS

FARMING
14.5 %

SERVICES
64.7%

Main Exports:

gold   silver   cacao

sugar   coffee beans   tobacco

National Holiday:
Independence Day (February 27)

Main Language:
Spanish

Form of Government:
presidential republic

Title for Country Leader:
president

OTHER
5%

RELIGION

ROMAN
CATHOLIC
95%

Unit of Money:
Dominican peso

GLOSSARY

artifacts—items made long ago by humans; artifacts tell people today about people from the past.

cuisine—a style of cooking

descendants—people related to a person or group of people who lived at an earlier time

diverse—made up of people or things that are different from one another

fertile—able to support growth

habitat—land with certain types of plants, animals, and weather

heritage—the traditions, achievements, and beliefs that are part of the history of a group of people

lagoons—shallow bodies of water that connect to a larger body of water

migrants—people who have moved to a new place for work or who have been forced to leave their home

native—originally from the area or related to a group of people that began in the area

patron saints—saints who are believed to look after a country or group of people

rural—related to the countryside

service jobs—jobs that perform tasks for people or businesses

slaves—people who work for no pay and are considered property

textile—a fabric that is woven or knit

thatched roofs—coverings made of grass or straw

tourists—people who travel to visit another place

traditions—customs, ideas, or beliefs handed down from one generation to the next

tropical—part of the tropics; the tropics is a hot, rainy region near the equator.

West Indies—the islands between southeastern North America and northern South America in the Caribbean Sea

TO LEARN MORE

AT THE LIBRARY

Cantor, Rachel Anne. *Dominican Republic*. New York, N.Y.: Bearport Publishing, 2016.

Díaz, Junot. *Islandborn*. New York, N.Y.: Dial Books for Young Readers, 2018.

Rechner, Amy. *Cuba*. Minneapolis, Minn.: Bellwether Media, 2019.

ON THE WEB

Learning more about the Dominican Republic is as easy as 1, 2, 3.

1. Go to www.factsurfer.com.

2. Enter "Dominican Republic" into the search box.

3. Click the "Surf" button and you will see a list of related web sites.

With factsurfer.com, finding more information is just a click away.

INDEX

activities, 20, 21
Alcázar de Colón, 4-5
capital (see Santo Domingo)
Carnival, 24
celebrations, 24-25
climate, 9, 20
communities, 14-15
customs, 16-17
education, 18
El Pañuelo (game), 21
fast facts, 28-29
food, 22-23
Gagá, 13, 25
Horford, Al, 13
housing, 14, 15
Independence Day, 24
landmarks, 4, 5
landscape, 8-9, 10
language, 12, 13, 17
location, 6-7
people, 5, 12-13, 17, 23
recipe, 23
religion, 13, 24, 25
Santo Domingo, 4, 7, 9,
    13, 15

Semana Santa, 25
size, 6
sports, 20
timeline, 26-27
transportation, 15
wildlife, 10-11
work, 15, 17, 19

The images in this book are reproduced through the courtesy of: Nick Hanna/ Alamy, front cover;
GiuseppeCrimeni, pp. 4-5, 20 (bottom); Luciano Ippolito, p. 5 (top); Zoran Karapancev, p. 5
(middle top); David Antonio Lopez Moya, pp. 5 (middle bottom), 13 (bottom); Don Mammoser, p. 5
(bottom); Evannovostro, p. 8; dibrova, p. 9 (top); saaton, p. 9 (bottom); Edvard Mizsei, p. 10 (top);
Tory Kallman, p. 10 (middle top); Reda & Co srl/ Alamy, p. 10 (middle bottom); Mirek Kijewski,
p. 10 (bottom); Werner Layer, p. 11; Christopher Booth/ Alamy, p. 12; Jonathan Daniel/ Getty,
p. 13 (top); cunfek, p. 14; Arcaid Images/ Alamy, p. 15; Robert John/ Alamy, p. 16; Klemen K. Misic,
p. 17; KIKE CALVO/ Alamy, p. 18; Ellen McKnight/ Alamy, p. 19 (top); Simon Rawles/ Alamy,
p. 19 (bottom); Corbis Documentary/ Getty, p. 20 (top); Cred:IlonaBudzbon, p. 21; Victor Gómez/
Alamy, p. 22; Clara Gonzalez, p. 23 (top); AS Food studio, p. 23 (middle); Ekaterina Kondratova,
p. 23 (bottom); Vova Pomortzeff/ Alamy, p. 24; Erika Santelicies/ Getty, p. 25; Michal Zalewski/
Wikipedia, p. 26 (top left); Prang Educational Co/ Wikipedia, p. 26 (top right); Peter Hermes Furian,
p. 26 (bottom); Richard/ Wikipedia, p. 27 (left); Dominican Republic government, 1933/ Wikipedia,
p. 27 (right); Robert Hackett, p. 29 (left); Fat Jackey, p. 29 (right).